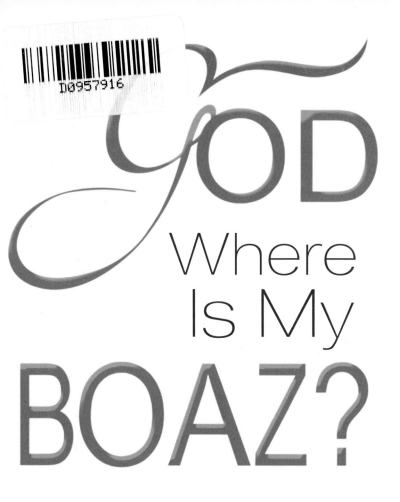

God
Where
Is My
BOAZ?

A woman's guide to understanding
what's hindering her from receiving
the man and love she desires.

Written by
Stephan Labossiere

God Where Is My Boaz, *Stephan Labossiere*

Copyright ©2013 by Stephan Labossiere

Published by Highly Favored Publishing

All scripture references used in this book can be found at: http://www.thebiblegateway.com.

Editor: C. Nzingha Smith

Formatted by: Ya Ya Ya Creative (yayayacreative@gmail.com)

First Edition: August 2013
Second Printing: 2015

ISBN No. 978-1493684861

PRINTED AND BOUND IN THE UNITED STATES OF AMERICA

Acknowledgements

First and foremost I would like to thank and acknowledge God for inspiring me to write this book. I had no plans on it until that faithful day that I felt overwhelmed by everything going on around me, and I wanted to quit my profession. It was in that moment of seeking God's guidance that I was led to creating *God Where Is My Boaz.* Being obedient has been a blessing, and it has allowed me to help more people. Listening to God has always been best. I also want to thank my mother who I love with all my heart. Her support and love has helped me greatly on this journey as I continue to embrace my passion and fulfill my purpose.

Dedication

This book is dedicated to every woman who genuinely desires true love in her life; who has ever had to deal with the struggle of waiting for or being in a relationship. I know it can get really tough, and my prayer is that every last one of you will be loved, respected, and cherished by the man who is truly best for you.

STEPHAN SPEAKS
real love.real talk.   real relatlonships.

Table of Contents

Introduction

Why? Why? Why? is God taking so long to send you a partner? I know you've had many frustrating moments trying to find the answer to this million dollar question! It simply doesn't make sense. Why do others continue to find relationships, while you wait (maybe not so patiently) for the one person God has for you? You're a good person at heart. You make time to worship and praise God. You may have even dedicated your life to God, by working in the church or ministry. So why is God being so dang stingy? It's about time He handed over that blessing and give you what you've been waiting for. After all, you don't have forever and this being single business isn't always as fun as advertised. Let's not even get started on being celibate. Hormones aren't always easy to keep in check, so this just needs to be resolved already. You want your Boaz and you want him NOW!

I have coached many clients with similar storylines. I remember one client who was forced to end a disappointing relationship. She was with the guy for five years, but in the end it just didn't work out. Like many women she became discouraged with relationships and more skeptical of trusting men. A believer in God, she decided to turn to Him for help. Her prayer; "God please send me my husband. Allow me to meet a good man that I can have a great relationship with. I can't deal with this anymore and I really need your help. Please send me the man I can finally spend the rest of my life with." You may have prayed a similar prayer in the past and can understand how this woman was feeling. Well, the very next day she went out and met an amazing man. He was good looking, had a good job, with no perceivable drama and he believed in God. The fact that she met him only a day after making her prayer request, led her to assume this was the man God had for her. The two of them got acquainted and started dating. Everything was going great and her belief was being validated 'in her mind' that she'd finally met her husband. To make a very long story short, it all fell apart three months later, when he found out she was waiting

Stephan Labossiere

until marriage to have sex. She couldn't believe it. She swore this man was sent straight from God as an answer to her prayers. "Everything was going so great", she thought. They had discussed their future together, but even so, it just wasn't enough once he realized access to the booty was denied. She was hurt and she wondered, how could God do this to her? Why did He set her up to be disappointed and once again alone? She was angry with God and didn't feel like she could trust Him or herself with love and relationships again. When she told me her story, the first question I asked her was: "did you ever ask God if this guy was the man He sent you, to confirm your assumption?" Her answer was no.

As some of you read the story, you became even more frustrated and discouraged because you can relate all too well. We've all had relationships we thought were going great; suddenly blow up in our faces. The reality is; when the pain and disappointment hits, the pain makes it harder to identify and acknowledge the real issues that led to the negative outcome of the relationship. We may begin to blame God. We may blame the other person or we may blame the circumstances in an attempt to find the reason why things didn't work out. However, many of us fail to look at ourselves in the mirror and truly evaluate how we contributed to the issues of our own relationships. We ignore our behavior. We choose to dwell on the negative aspects of the experience because we refuse to embrace the lessons that we need to learn.

Our individual actions play a huge part in the result of our relationships. Many times a better approach means a much better result. This principle applies with God also, as we hope to receive the blessings He has for us. Some people believe the blessing will come, if it's meant, no matter what they do. My response to them; read and embrace *James* 2:14-17, which essentially states, *"Faith without works is dead."* There may be specific actions you have to take to receive the blessing. These actions can only be revealed when you take the time to ask God what needs to be done.

In this book, I'm going to help bring clarity to the internal struggle you've been enduring. I've been led to provide insight into the things hindering your progression in relationships. For some, these issues have completely paralyzed you

Stephan Labossiere

and have hindered you from receiving the many blessings you deserve in life. I've experienced many thing spiritually and I've seen first-hand what many other women as well as men have gone through. As a friend, relative and certified relationship coach, I've had the opportunity to deeply examine many people's lives. As a result, I've been able to discover the issues many people tend to overlook in their own struggles. I've observed, I've prayed and now I want to bring these issues to light. My hope is to genuinely help you along your journey to the love and life you desire. Before I continue I want to state a few facts you should keep in mind as you read:

#1— I Am Not God.

Ok, I think it's pretty obvious, but there is a point I'm trying to make here. I'm hand delivering a message to you, for your benefit, by providing the insight you may need to receive your breakthrough. I'm the messenger, not the creator of the message. No matter how precisely the things in this book connect with your situation and hit home for you, DO NOT overlook the very important next step: Go to God in prayer and verify that I'm speaking to you from the right place. You should pray for confirmation and identify which issues you need to address and the approach to take to resolve the issues. Never rely solely on what someone tells you. Your Father wants to speak directly to you through prayer.

#2 — You Are Not Alone.

Whether you realize it or not, there are a lot of people who struggle with the issues presented in this book. However, some people aren't always forthcoming about having these issues. They don't feel they can openly share what they're going through with others. Even though these issues are emphasized by our churches and society to relate more with women, do not be mistaken, there are plenty of men who are fighting these same battles as well. Understand that many other people feel your pain and understand what you're going through. We should encourage each other and accept the truth about what we have to face, working together to get to our rightful destinations.

#3 — I'm Not Here to Judge.
I'm Here to Help.

I want to encourage everyone reading this book to do so with an open mind. I don't want you to feel as if I'm attacking you, talking down to you, or negatively criticizing you. I'm just as flawed as anyone. This book is about being able to truly self-evaluate ourselves and address the real issues that exist underneath the surface. Issues you have ignored or dismissed altogether for way too long. This book is about providing you with a new perspective. This new perspective will give you an understanding of the next steps needed to transform your life and your relationships. Some information will apply to you and some won't. Identify the information that applies to you, and decide to take the necessary steps to eliminate anything that's holding you back. I speak to you out of love and the shared struggle of trying to become the individual God has designed us to be. Once we know who we are in God, the doors open and we are able to receive the things and the person truly best for us.

#4 — God Doesn't Want You to Have Any "Man". He Wants You to Have *The* Man Who is Truly *Best* For You.

I can give you all the tips and tricks on how to get you a man, but that isn't what this book is about. I've seen plenty of women try to take shortcuts to companionship, only to end up on the highway to heartbreak. God wants the best for you and anything of great value requires great effort. There's work to be done and that work begins within you. God wants the relationship you receive to glorify Him and to keep His child (you) in a place of great love and fulfillment.

No more quick fixes. No more running from the problems. We all struggle to face them, but not facing them only makes matters worse. With this book, you will be able to climb and conquer your mountain(s) and begin moving in a more positive direction. With that said let's begin by getting a better understanding of why God still hasn't sent you your Boaz.

The Story of
Ruth & Boaz

You may be familiar with the biblical story of Ruth, a young woman who married a great man named Boaz. Ruth's story is used by many churches as a reference to speak about the man God has in store for many women of God. Rather than give you a reprint of the entire book of Ruth here, I'll give you a brief summary accompanied by supporting scripture. Having the background of the story will give you a true understanding as to how everything happened and how Ruth ended up with Boaz. Here goes...

Ruth and her sister Orpah were married to two brothers who died. Their mother-in-law, Naomi had also lost her husband around the same time. Depression overtook Naomi at the massive

"when you do what you're supposed to do, you'll get what you're supposed to get."

loss of her sons and husband. Naomi urged both Ruth and Orpah to return to their homeland, to save themselves from starvation and ultimately to seek a better life for themselves by remarrying. After some emotional back and forth Orpah headed back home, but Ruth stayed and vowed not to leave Naomi no matter what. Together Naomi and Ruth traveled from Moab to Bethlehem. The women had to figure out how they were going to survive alone without husbands. *Ruth 2:2 states; "And Ruth the Moabite said to Naomi, 'Let me go to the fields and pick up the leftover grain behind anyone in whose eyes I find favor.'"* When Ruth goes out to gather in the fields, she ends up in the field belonging to a wealthy man named, Boaz. Boaz notices Ruth and questions his workers to find out who she is. This part of the story is often misinterpreted and presented as a fairytale encounter of love at first sight; however continue to read and you will see this isn't the case at all. Ruth had to put in some work to win Boaz over.

[6] The overseer replied, "She is the Moabite who came back from Moab with Naomi.
[7] She said, "Please let me glean and gather among the sheaves behind the harvesters." She came into the field and has remained

here from morning till now, except for a short rest in the shelter." [8] So Boaz said to Ruth, "My daughter, listen to me. Don't go and glean in another field and don't go away from here. Stay here with the women who work for me. [9] Watch the field where the men are harvesting, and follow along after the women. I have told the men not to lay a hand on you. And whenever you are thirsty, go and get a drink from the water jars the men have filled."

What are you thinking? Let me guess; you're thinking 'he must really like her'. After all it seems like he's truly showing interest in her. He's also providing for her and/or courting her as a real man should. Let's continue. Ruth was so flattered by his gesture that she had to ask:

[10] "Why have I found such favor in your eyes that you notice me—a foreigner?" [11] Boaz replied, "I've been told all about what you have done for your mother-in-law since the death of your husband—how you left your father and mother and your homeland and came to live with a people you did not know before. [12] May the LORD repay you for what you have done. May you be richly rewarded

by the LORD, the God of Israel, under whose wings you have come to take refuge."

Did you see what just happened? Many interpret Ruth's story in a way that makes it seem like Boaz just saw Ruth, wanted her and started to make his move. Wrong. In actuality Boaz respected and recognized Ruth's character first. As a result he held her in high regard. You can instantly catch a man's attention, but if you don't have his respect you won't get the relationship you deserve. Let's continue.

Ruth went back to her mother-in-law and told her all of the good news. Naomi was so happy she asked Ruth whose field she was gleaning in. Ruth told her the field belonged to a man named Boaz. Naomi knew Boaz, he was her close relative. Because Naomi and Boaz were related, this made him their "guardian redeemer" which in those days was a legal term for, "one who has the obligation to redeem a relative in serious difficulty." So Ruth continued gleaning in Boaz's field when one day Naomi says to her.

Ruth 3: "My daughter, I must find a home for you, where you will be well provided for.

² Now Boaz, with whose women you have worked, is a relative of ours. Tonight he will be winnowing barley on the threshing floor. ³ Wash, put on perfume, and get dressed in your best clothes. Then go down to the threshing floor, but don't let him know you are there until he has finished eating and drinking. ⁴ When he lies down, note the place where he is lying. Then go and uncover his feet and lie down. He will tell you what to do."

⁷ When Boaz had finished eating and drinking and was in good spirits, he went over to lie down at the far end of the grain pile. Ruth approached quietly, uncovered his feet and lay down. ⁸ In the middle of the night something startled the man; he turned—and there was a woman lying at his feet! ⁹ "Who are you?" he asked. "I am your servant Ruth," she said. "Spread the corner of your garment over me, since you are a guardian redeemer of our family."

Boaz replies: ¹⁰ "The Lord bless you, my daughter," he replied. "This kindness is greater than that which you showed earlier: You have not run after the younger men, whether rich or poor. ¹¹ And now, my daughter, don't be afraid. I will do for you all you ask. All the people of my town know that you are a woman of noble character. [12] Although it is true that I am a guardian-redeemer of our family, there is another who is more closely related than I. [13] Stay here for the night and in the morning if he wants to do his duty as your guardian-redeemer, good; let him redeem you. But if he is not willing, as surely as the LORD lives I will do it. Lie here until morning."

Notice again the mention of Ruth's great character and the respect he has for her. That is a huge reason why this situation works out for Ruth. Some people use this part of the story to try to justify their theory of why women should propose to men. However, if you give it a closer look, Ruth never asks Boaz to marry her. She really doesn't ask him anything at all. She simply states who she is to him and he understands his duty in this situation. Ruth had the law of the land on her side. No woman in the 21st century can walk up to a man and say "hey, I'm your wife and you need to marry me" without getting the side eye or being laughed at in most cases. Trying to relate the two still isn't the same. The story continues with Boaz speaking to the other close relative and they agreed on Boaz remaining the 'guardian redeemer' for his family. Boaz also stays true to his word and marries Ruth. It was important to highlight specific parts of Ruth's story because many women misrepresent the meaning of the story and miss the valuable lessons God reveals to women on the process of meeting your Boaz.

Lesson #1:

Stop "waiting" for Boaz. Ruth never sat back and just waited for things to happen. She was proactive and didn't wait for Boaz to initiate things with her. She followed a two-step principle all women should remember: prepare and position yourself. She was already prepared and had the mindset of a wife when she met Boaz. *Proverbs 18:22* states: *"Whoso findeth a wife, findeth a good thing"* not *"he who findeth a woman who wishes to be married."* Ruth already embodied the role she wanted to hold. It's like when they tell you to dress for the position you want at work. If you hold back and don't present yourself as someone who is right for the position, you may never get that promotion.

Lesson #2:

You have to put yourself out there. This speaks to the second half of the above principle; position yourself. Many women feel a man should approach them if he's interested. They believe nothing will stop him from pursuing them, if they are in fact what he really wants. Problem is ladies; he doesn't know you yet, so how can he truly know he wants you? I'm not saying I believe women should "pursue" and chase after men. In my coaching session entitled, *"He Needs to Come to You: Why and How This Isn't Always True,"* I teach in great detail how important it is that a woman makes herself more approachable and known to the man she desires. If not, she may find herself choosing from a much less desirable pool of men.

Ultimately the one thing missing from Ruth's story in my opinion was a conversation with God. Seeking God's guidance will help you sort through the men that are simply a waste of your time. Women have great intuition for the most part, but many do not embrace it as they should when it comes to selecting the men they date. As a woman of God I believe intuition grows stronger. However, it serves no purpose if you're going to try and convince yourself of reasons why you should go against your gut feelings and disregard the warning signs. Prepare and position yourself are two important things to remember as you begin to discover other obstacles that may be hindering you from getting the man and love you deserve. You can start with the language you use. Stop saying "I'm waiting for my Boaz," change it to, "I'm preparing for my Boaz."

Further Insight

#1: If scripture says, "He that findeth a wife" then why are you encouraging women to position themselves and initiate things with a man?

"To find" does not mean you have to make the man search for you literally. By definition, "to find" also means: To come upon, often by accident; meet with. If you make the process of crossing paths and engaging with you difficult, you might cheat yourself out of an opportunity for something great. Always remember that showing interest in a man is not the same as chasing after him.

#2: You say it's important to have the man's respect, but a lot of men just don't respect women in general. What can I really do about that with all the negativity that exists in society towards women?

When respect is demanded from a man (properly) respect is given. Unfortunately, many women sell themselves short and accept less than what they deserve because they want companionship so badly. Doing this only causes the man to lose respect. As a result the woman feels unhappy and unfulfilled. If you're being the woman God wants you to be and a man still doesn't respect you, surely that isn't the man God has for you. Always hold to the standard of respect you deserve and a great man will easily recognize the caliber of woman you are and treat you accordingly.

#3: How does a woman prepare to be a wife? What exactly should I be doing?

Focus on getting aligned with where God wants you to be in life. It doesn't mean you have to be perfect. You will have your 'moments'. What it means is you'll be moving forward on the path God has for you and not the path that you've chosen based on your own logic. To accomplish this you have to make time to connect with God through prayer. You have to understand everyone has a different path to walk and therefore your preparation may be different from other people you know. Your preparation will include making sure you have healed from past hurts and embraced your true value and potential as a woman. Your preparation is a process and it's all about becoming and being the woman God has truly designed you to be.

You Must Forgive & Heal,
Then You Can Love

[4] "Love is patient and kind; love does not envy or boast; it is not arrogant [5] or rude. It does not insist on its own way; it's not irritable or resentful; [6] it does not rejoice at wrongdoing, but rejoices with the truth. [7] Love bears all things, believes all things, hopes all things, and endures all things."

1 Corinthians 13:4-7 NKJ

A young female college student came to me for advice regarding her direction in life; spiritually, professionally, and romantically. We talked about school and what she hoped to achieve in her professional life. When we started talking about men and relationships, her attitude changed from optimistic to skeptical. I had to dig below the surface to find out why she had such a negative outlook on men and relationships. What I found was the young woman had experienced a childhood without her father around. The pain still lingered and hindered her ability to open up her heart to love. Not-to-mention the heartbreak she experienced earlier in her college years. She really liked a guy and wanted to be in a serious relationship with him. He was viewed by many as a "player" and knew the right things to say to make her feel like it'd be different with her. She felt she could give him the benefit of the doubt and proceeded to get closer to him. Eventually a sexual relationship developed and next thing she knew, the guy was in a relationship with another girl. She was hurt. Her unresolved pain turned into anger, the anger turned into an unwillingness to embrace having serious feelings for any other man.

> **" A father's love teaches a girl how a man's love should feel. "**

Here's how I helped her forgive and heal, so she could love again. The first step was to help her address her past issues dealing with her father's absence. Many times a woman can find herself latching on to the wrong kind of man because she's never experienced a healthy loving relationship with a man before. The initial example should come from a father/daughter relationship. A father's love teaches a girl how a man's love should feel. A father's love, protects, provides security and let's her know she's valued. Not having her father's love, the young lady had no foundation and this left her extremely fragile in her relationships with men. She needed to express her feelings to her father directly. I explained to her that getting things off her chest would be a great relief and would help her with the process of her forgiving & healing so she could move on to love. So she did and she noted how much of a weight was lifted off of her shoulders as a result. Holding pain and hurt inside is unhealthy and locks in a lot of toxic energy that works against what we really want, which is healthy love. After the initial step was completed, even though she had more work to do and more lessons to learn, she was now on her way to identifying the other obstacles standing in her way of the love and life she deserved and desired.

It's really difficult to love the way the scripture instructs us to. In fact, it's impossible to love the way the scripture instructs us to without God's help. When we constantly worry about being taken advantage of, when we remember how deeply the last person hurt us, we do our best to guard against experiencing that type of pain again. Any logical human being would proceed with caution and take steps to "protect their hearts". However, God doesn't operate by logic and His love has no limits. He doesn't want us to protect our hearts from getting hurt. He wants us to trust Him to guard our hearts. God wants us to protect our hearts from being infected with anger, fear, lust, and anything else negative that can knock us off our path and distance us from His love. So how do we manage to do this considering all the bad relationships we've been through and the pain and hurt they left behind? Here's how:

#1— Forgive Those Who Hurt You and Forgive Yourself.

You can't be expected to forget, but it's always in your best interest to forgive. Holding on to the pain people have caused you will make it much harder, if not impossible, to heal and be able to love. Hurt people, hurt people. In most (if not all) cases the person that did you wrong was a damaged individual who hadn't addressed their own issues. Don't continue the cycle! Also, don't overlook the need to forgive yourself. We have all made mistakes. Holding past mistakes over your own head will certainly hinder you from getting what you deserve, which is love. Don't remain in bondage to the negative energy produced by past pain and disappointment. Let forgiveness be your freedom.

#2 — Take Your Time and Don't Rush Into Anything.

Being single can be a great experience when you embrace it as an opportunity to heal and grow. Jumping from relationship to relationship or always being in a rush to find one, doesn't give you the time you need for yourself. Time to yourself is extremely essential when you still have unaddressed issues from past relationships. It's like an athlete rushing back to play after an injury. If she comes back too quickly, she's at a much higher risk of repeat injury. Even if she plays, say on a bad ankle (a bad heart in regards to relationships), she won't be playing at her full potential. That's basically what it boils down to. You should be patient with the healing process. Make sure you do a full rehabilitation on your heart so that it can truly operate at the level God intended.

#3 — Truly Embrace Giving and Receiving Love.

Without completing the above two steps, you will continue to struggle with giving and receiving love. This applies to loving others and more importantly loving yourself. You may be walking around carrying with you a lot of negative energy, which leads to protective walls being erected in your life,

> **"Complete healing comes through God..."**

consciously or unconsciously. The same walls you think you're using to protect yourself are the same walls blocking your blessings. How can God release the love you deserve, in the form of a life partner, if you continue to restrict love from properly flowing in and out of you? It's hard to embrace the idea of being vulnerable, which is why it can be very hard embracing love. Complete healing comes through God and is absolutely necessary to truly overcome the obstacle of un-forgiveness once and for all. Forgiving and healing will help you position yourself properly for love and happiness.

Many women try to ignore the need for forgiveness and complete healing, but it always comes back to haunt them one way or another. Sometimes we'll say we've forgiven someone, but take a deeper look and make sure you didn't just try to move past the issue without really addressing it. You can't overcome an obstacle unless you are willing to face it head on. Don't run away from the issue(s). If you need help (friend, family, or a professional) don't be afraid or ashamed to ask for the assistance you need. It may be a tough mountain to climb but doing so will help you reach new heights.

Further Insight

#1: If I'm dealing with past pain do I really need to have a conversation with the person that hurt me? Can't I just forgive them on my own and move on?

In many cases people have a lot on their chest they need to unload. I feel it's best to express how you feel directly to the person that hurt you. This can be by phone, by email, or snail mail, whatever method you feel is best and are most comfortable with. Talking about the situation and pain openly with the source of the issue can be very refreshing. A weight will be lifted off your shoulders and you're able to get rid of the toxic energy in your system. It doesn't mean the person

> **"Forgiveness is all about you."**

will be receptive, it doesn't mean the energy will be transferred into guilt or that they will take any steps toward righting their wrong. Forgiveness is all about you. If the person isn't available for you to reach out to directly, the act of writing the situation out or speaking to someone you trust about it can still provide the release needed.

#2: I made a choice to forgive the people who have hurt me but I can't seem to forget or completely move past it. Thinking about it still makes me so upset and puts me in a very negative mindset?

Forgiveness is a continual process. We need God's help as I mentioned earlier in the chapter. It's not something you should try to do by your own strength or power. We have to practice forgiveness continually by not dwelling in those negative moments whenever they arise and if needed, by forgiving the people who hurt us as often as needed until the negative emotions surrounding the situation are no longer present. Tell yourself what's done is done and choose to focus on moving forward in a positive and loving way. In time it will get easier and you won't allow any negative emotions to consume you. Also make sure you have taken the above steps to get things off of your chest so you can begin the process of complete healing.

#3: *Proverbs 4:23* says "a person should guard their hearts." So what is so wrong with having walls up and avoiding being hurt by people?

I believe this is a misinterpreted scripture. "Guard your heart" doesn't mean you have to walk around with walls, barbwire and land mines around your heart to keep it from being hurt. If you have that much security surrounding your heart you will not only keep the bad guys out, you'll also make it a struggle for the man who is actually for you to make it through. God doesn't want you operating in fear but in faith. When you seek God's clearance on the men in your life, you can trust Him with the process. Otherwise you will simply set yourself up for failure.

Your Way Isn't
God's Way

⁵"Trust in the LORD with all your heart and lean not on your own understanding; ⁶ in all your ways submit to him, and he will make your paths straight."
Proverbs 3:5-6

A middle aged woman shared her personal story of relationship frustration with me while attending an event I was speaking at. She made the decision many years ago to give her life to God and break away from her previous lifestyle. She wanted to "do better" and she also wanted a husband she could share her life with. She concluded it would be best for her to join a church and become devoted to spending her time there serving God. With this approach she would be a "good Christian" and what better place to find a "good Christian" man, right?

Well ten years passed her by and she was still in the church on a regular basis and still very single.

She expressed her frustration and confusion as to why taking this route had yet to produce the results she was hoping for. She would speak to her pastor and other members of the church about the issue but all the advice they offered was for her to continue to pray and be patient. I asked her if she had determined if this was the best route for her to take or if she actually took time to ask God, which route she should go. When answering the question, she realized she had never taken the time to ask God for direction. She thought she was doing the right thing and couldn't see why this would be a bad choice.

Everyone is created to serve in some form of ministry, but was serving in the four walls of the church truly her appointed area? We often want things to fit inside our logic and comfort zone but it doesn't always work that way. So here are a few things to be mindful of when trying to avoid finding yourself in this same position.

#1 — God's Path to Your Blessing May Not Always Make Sense.

The closer your relationship is with God, the more you will see that things won't always make sense at first. God may direct you to do things that just don't add up in your mind. However, those who are obedient often end up seeing how things can and will work out better than they expected in the end. Our logic can sometimes get us in trouble. Be mindful not to give logic so much power over what you feel in your spirit/intuition. This principle directly applies to the area of being blessed with a man you can share your life with as well.

#2 — Just Because He Looks Good Doesn't Mean He's the Man From God.

Don't be so quick to assume the great guy that came into your life at the "right time" is God's answer to your prayers for a husband. I'm not saying he isn't, but jumping to premature conclusions can get you into a lot of trouble. I always say; "people should be careful of only looking for signs from God." Remember the Devil can put up billboards too. We tend to get too caught up in what we see and many times this is merely a distraction from the things we should be looking at. That guy could be a great man but that doesn't make him the right man for you.

#3 — It Never Hurts To Verify.

Considering my first two points above, it can be difficult to really know when you're on the right track in regards to where God wants you to be in your life and with whom. We are all human so mistakes are natural and easy to make. To help eliminate some of these mistakes and common misinterpretations, you should make time to verify through prayer, what God wants you to know and do regarding your relationships. Some of you will say, "God doesn't speak to you directly", so you rely on other means of communication (dreams, signs, etc). No matter your method, there are always ways to get confirmation from God. There is consistency in the truth and confusion in lies. Remember that.

> "Faith is based on believing in things unseen."

As the proverb states; *"lean not on your understanding"*, we have to be careful not to follow the habit of relying so heavily on our logic, which is limited and instead we should be tapping into spiritual discernment. Faith is based on believing in things unseen. We have to be willing and able to embrace what God is revealing to us spiritually even when everything on the surface looks like a complete mess. Our eyes, ears, and heart can deceive us, but God is always able to lead us in the right direction.

Further Insight

#1: If something proves to clearly not be for me, wouldn't it be a bad decision to still hold on and try to overlook the obvious negatives?

Typically the answer is yes. However, when God is in it, this isn't always the case. Sometimes what looks bad is for your good and only temporary. A reaction based solely off what you see will only prolong the situation and make it worse. Whenever there is any uncertainty or reason to pause out of cautiousness, then I encourage you to take a moment if you haven't already to get God's input on the situation. Women's intuition speaks loud and clear; when something isn't right or when something isn't what it appears to be. Listen to your inner voice, to your intuition, to your heart and to God and make sure there is a consensus on the matter before you begin or proceed any further.

#2: What happens when I meet a great guy and he tells me that God told him I am his wife? Should I believe him or is this some sort of warning sign that he is trying to play me?

I can go to any woman right now and claim God told me she's my wife, but that doesn't make the claim true. Players and con-artist come in all shapes and sizes including the supposed "man of God" character. So do not just take a man's word for it. You should have your own relationship with God that allows you to pray and seek His answer to the claim of you being "wifey". You will be able to truly feel it, if he is the man for you and if you truly are his wife. Keep in mind the fact that some men may not be blatantly trying to pull one over on you. Some men may be misguided and simply going off a desire of the flesh rather than a message from their Spirit. Then there are men who truly feel within them that you are their wife and their intentions are not bad in any way. Either way, seek guidance from God to gain the clarity you need in this type of situation before you proceed and jump into anything serious.

#3: I pray to God regularly, but I don't get direct answers from Him. Sometimes I feel like I don't get any answers at all. How should I handle not knowing what to do in a specific situation?

Whenever someone asks me this question, I always answer them by asking; "is it that He hasn't answered you or is it that you aren't listening or accepting the answer He's given you?" Often times we are looking for answers in the midst of chaos and countless distractions. This makes it very hard to hear God clearly. I recommend taking a moment to quiet yourself and do your best to remove all the "outside" noise. Take some time by yourself and consider going on a fast. The fast doesn't always have to only include food and water. Fasting is about sacrificing something you consider vital in your daily routine that could be considered a distraction from you hearing from God. Giving it up for a set amount of time should free up time for you to spend time praying and focusing on God in peace. Many women have gained the clarity they needed by going on a fast and I believe it's a great thing to do. In addition to fasting and I don't want to sound like a broken record here, but trust your intuition. Women often make decisions based on their emotions and/or logic and ignore their intuition/Spirit, which in fact gives them the correct answer on what to do. Don't ignore the God given gift of discernment you as women have been blessed with.

You Expect God to Deliver a Man to Your Doorstep

¹⁴ What does it profit, my brethren, if someone says he has faith but does not have works? Can faith save him? ¹⁵ If a brother or sister is naked and destitute of daily food, ¹⁶ and one of you says to them, "Depart in peace, be warmed and filled," but you do not give them the things which are needed for the body, what does it profit? ¹⁷ Thus also faith by itself, if it does not have works, is dead.

James 2:14-26

I have a saying I say all the time: "God is not FedEx®". We shouldn't expect to place an order through prayer and have our prayers answered and delivered to our doorstep with little to no effort on our part. Sure, God is able to do whatever He wants, however He wants, and sometimes He will make it that simple. I just personally don't think God wants us to expect Him to use this route every time or view Him as FedEx.

Strength and character are built through adversity. We're able to learn the lessons we need and grow, when we put ourselves in the vulnerable position of taking action. So when receiving the blessing of a husband you shouldn't think that this principle will go away and not apply to you.

> "Strength and character are built through adversity."

You may have heard another woman say this before; "I'm waiting on God to bring me my spouse." Honestly, even I've said it and it feels like a very safe and correct statement to make. The truth is it can be a dangerous one, depending on how you approach the situation. If waiting on God means; you're going to focus on what He wants you to focus on and trust His timing, then you're in good shape. If the statement means; you're going to do whatever makes sense to you because God will figure out a way to drop this person in your lap, then you should reconsider your perspective.

It's very easy to use the, I'm waiting on God explanation as a way to avoid dealing with our deeper issues. This explanation explains away the deeper issues that may be at play underneath the surface, either knowingly or unconsciously. You may not always be forthcoming or be willing to embrace what is truly playing into your lackadaisical approach to finding/receiving your Boaz. Here are some possible explanations to why you may be holding on to this perspective:

#1— You're Too Worn Down From Past Experiences.

Let's face it; relationships can get really rough sometimes. Regardless of whether our attempts are misguided or not, we still feel the sting of disappointment when things don't work out as well as we hoped. The more life you live, the more of these moments you've likely experienced or will experience. This can lead to emotional, mental, and spiritual fatigue, which hinders your ability to take the necessary steps for progress and change for the better. God gave us all the ability to overcome our issues and we should seek His guidance on the best approach to take to be successful at overcoming them. The best approach to your healing could involve fasting and prayer to clear your mind and gain clarity into your situation as I mentioned earlier. There also may be too many unnecessary distractions and obligations in your life. Identifying and removing them can help bring about more peace in your life. Also be mindful that your eating and sleeping habits can contribute to increased fatigue and an inability to deal with the things life throws at you. Improving your diet and adding an exercise regimen to your daily routine can help give you the boost you need also. Take the steps to evaluate and implement the correct adjustments you need to make so fatigue doesn't continue to paralyze you.

#2 — You're Trying to Avoid Getting Hurt.

In addition to being worn down, you may simply be afraid to open up and try. Fear is always present and it will try to grip us and hinder us from love. We must be willing to acknowledge fear for what it is. Nobody likes having their feelings hurt or their hearts broken. However, the possibility will always exist when we're dealing with other people in relationships. You may have reached a point where you don't trust your own judgment and want God to make all your decisions for you. The problem with this; no matter what God does, that same fear of being hurt will get in the way of you embracing what He has for you. God can't stop you from choosing to run from a situation or person that has you feeling overwhelmed. You have to decide to take a stand against fear. Only you can make the choice to overcome your fears. *"God does not give us a spirit of fear, but of power, love and a sound mind." 2 Timothy 1:7 NLT.*

#3 — There's Someone You're Already In Love With.

You may be sitting back, not doing much about your love life because you're already in love with and have met your Boaz. However, there's a problem; it's very difficult to tell people your heart still yearns for someone who you've not been able to be with right now (for various reasons). Rather than deal with the questions and pressure from others to *let it go*, you decide not to take action in finding a partner. You choose to hide behind any explanation you can give, that will make others back off the subject of why you're still single. The explanations and

"The truth shall set you free..."

excuses won't change the fact that your heart is with a person right now who you are not currently with. This needs to be addressed or you may find yourself stuck in an undesirable cycle. The truth shall set you free but continuing to hide behind a lie only keeps you in bondage.

If you're trying to reach a destination you have to put forth the effort to; walk, drive, fly or use some other mode of transportation in order to get there. To arrive there in good time, your best bet is to get some good directions. God has the GPS for our lives. Who better to go to than Him? Unless God is telling you to be still, don't overlook the need for you to take action. Instead of using God as a crutch, use him as a guide. We all know how tough it can be to fight through the negative, but it's just part of the process. Your growth as a person depends on the process itself and the lessons God wants you to learn to grow and mature. In order to grow, we have to keep pushing forward, toward His desired end. Your blessing is there waiting for you. Now, you just need to get up and go get it, using God's guidance.

Further Insight

#1: I'm tired and don't feel like dealing with any of this. It seems like it's too much and I've been in this battle for so long. How do I muster up the strength to keep pushing forward?

As I explained earlier in this chapter, life can be very draining and we all experience moments and phases where we don't believe we have the energy to keep going in our pursuits in life and love. When we get here, we have to learn to take a break and make some alone time for ourselves. When we don't take the necessary breaks, we relinquish our ability to take control of the situation, we become victims. We have to structure our lives in a way that provides more peace and gives us the ability to recharge our batteries. What a person needs specifically will vary based on the individual, but ultimately you just have to sit down and create a better structure in your life. Avoid waiting until you're burnt out to make changes. Implement changes as often as needed e.g., daily, weekly, or monthly routines that alleviate the stress and fatigue and help you relax. Some women enjoy a spa day once a month. Others create a section in their home for quiet time and relaxation. Setting aside time for an exercise regimen can also give you an extra boost and help you de-stress. It may seem hard, but it can be done and when you accomplish this, you will gain the energy you need to press forward.

#2: You've mentioned how running from getting hurt and putting walls up are counterproductive multiple times in this book so far. It seems this is a point you truly want to drive home. What can I do to win the battle over the fear and temptation to run when I feel overwhelmed?

Good observation. I've definitely highlighted this point as much as possible throughout the book because it's a vital part of success in life and in your relationships. I have seen firsthand how fear of getting hurt has played out in the lives of so many women and men's lives. The result of acting on this fear is that many women end up not being with a man they truly love and not pursuing the dreams they are truly passionate about. When we allow fear to dictate our actions, we've consequently handed our control over to the Devil and we all know this isn't best. So when you are evaluating a situation ask yourself; "am I going to let the Devil or God motivate me in making this decision? Will I let fear or faith, have its way?" Basically, that's what it boils down to. I believe looking at it that way will help push you more towards faith. Also, know there is more that's involved, like addressing past issues and seeking God's guidance on specific matters. Sometimes God wants you to step away and other times He may want you to hit the issues head on. Go to God in prayer for guidance in every situation you face, so you know what's best for you.

#3: Ok, so let's say I'm in love with a man I'm not currently in a relationship with. If the reason we aren't together is his doing am I really expected to wait to wait on him? Shouldn't I just move on and wait for God to send me another man that will embrace being with me?

You are never expected to wait on a man but you may be expected to wait on God. Sometimes it's the right guy, but the wrong time. God may need you and Him to go through a process first before He can bring you two into a successful relationship together. That's why you have to find out from God what you need to be doing right now. Many people rush into the arms of someone else only to create a bigger mess of the situation. Not to mention, making this decision pulls innocent by-standards who now find themselves with a person whose heart is truly with someone else. The interesting thing is people who have a strong, deep connection tend to eventually find their way back to each other. It then becomes an issue of how many more obstacles have you added during the waiting period, because you acted impulsively and impatiently. Not properly dealing with your impatience concerning your companionship, often ends in disaster. What you do while you wait, can be the difference between finally being with the person you truly love or prolonging the love you truly deserve.

You're Too Occupied With
The Wrong Man

"Forget the former things; do not dwell on
the past. See, I am doing a new thing! Now
it springs up; do you not perceive it?"
Isaiah 43:18-19

Being single can be a blessing in disguise,
even though it may feel at times like it
sucks. During the down moments of
singlehood, we sometimes latch on to the wrong
person looking for companionship. This can
happen via casual acquaintances, friends with
benefits, committed relationships (at least you
hope it's committed), and dare I even say it, even
with marriage. Yes, just because you reached the
altar, doesn't mean you got there with the person
that is truly best for you. Nor
does it mean you did it for the
right reasons or with the best
intentions. You may still be
missing the relationship blessing

**"Fear can
paralyze
us..."**

that's truly for you. After all, how can you make any progress, when the path is blocked by your pre-occupation with the wrong person? Some may not like the fact I included marriage in the mix, but the principle remains the same. If the relationship wasn't brought together under God's guidance, then it shouldn't come as a huge surprise when the relationship fails and the man is unable to give you the love and fulfillment you desire.

Fear can paralyze us as I've mentioned previously. Even when we know deep inside to, *let a relationship go*, we often find ourselves struggling to make the move to leave the relationship. It's always easier for us on the outside of the relationship, to tell a person they need to walk away. However, many of us make the same mistakes when placed in the same position. What's contributing to the hold this person seems to have on you? Why do you try to convince yourself of reasons you have to stay with him, when you know in your heart the relationship isn't best for you? We have to be honest with ourselves if we are going to break free from this type of bondage. Here are a few reasons why you may continue to hold on to the wrong person after realizing he's not for you:

#1 — You're Too Scared To Be Alone.

For many of you, the thought of being alone makes you extremely uncomfortable. You've decided it's better to have a piece of someone, than to have no one at all. The problem with this reasoning; you're selling yourself short. The feeling of loneliness has pushed a lot of people into the arms of the wrong person and keeps them there. Being by yourself causes you to have to face yourself. When you have yet to truly learn and embrace who you are, being alone is like spending time with a stranger and that can be scary. Self-evaluation is a difficult process for a lot of people and they would much rather find a way to distract themselves from it. Using relationships to escape your reality however, will only make things worse. You have to stop viewing being single as the plague. Do not allow others to make you feel less valued because "you don't have a man." Family, friends, and society as a whole can many times make you feel bad about not being in a relationship or on the hunt for a relationship every moment of your life. I encourage you to resist this perspective, or allow it to get the best of you. Rushing to be with someone or getting into a relationship prematurely in order to appease others will leave you paying the consequences. Also note, the man you're with doesn't have to be no-good in order for him not to be right for you. Even if you have a "good guy", he just might not be the one for you. You know this because even though you're with him, you still feel something missing within your relationship. So don't do it! Remember that being single is an opportunity for you to learn, grow, and be available for the relationship and man you truly deserve.

#2 — You Struggle To Walk Away Because Of The Time And Energy Already Invested.

It's never easy to walk away from a person you've made a large time and emotional investment in. In fact, some of you will stop at nothing to get a return on that investment. You fight to keep this person in your life, not realizing all you're doing is wasting more energy and time, when you know deep inside it's not where you belong. You can walk away now or you can cause more damage to yourself and the other person by staying longer. It's not that I'm against trying to work things out, but you have to be honest with yourself and ask God; "is this truly the person I should be in a relationship with?" If the answer is no, don't let pride, frustration, or any other negative emotion keep you there any longer. You will not get a return on your investment. Cut your losses and move on to bigger and better things.

#3 — Not Wanting To Admit You Made A Bad Choice.

Being wrong about your relationship choices is never a good feeling. It stings and it's something we try not to recognize for as long as we can avoid it. You gave yourself every reason to believe the relationship could and would work and you continue to hang on to the illusion for dear life. You're waiting to have the choices you made validated up to this point so you can justify your reasons to stay in the relationship. You want to feel valued by this man you poured into and gave so much of yourself to. However, you won't change anything by trying to force the issue with someone who simply isn't the man for you. Understand that we all make mistakes. Understand that if you went into this relationship without consulting God then you know the step you missed in the process. Don't let the fact that you fought so hard to prove to others you were in the right place, stop you from acknowledging you're in the wrong place. There are a lot of other reasons people hold on to bad relationships.

❖ You are repeating the cycle of your parents.

❖ Kids may be involved and you feel it's better to stay together.

❖ You don't feel like you can do any better.

❖ You may be scared for your life due to mental and physical abuse.

"Get the help you need to break away from these unhealthy attachments."

No matter the reason, the principle remains the same; the longer you hold on to a person who isn't for you, the longer you will go without receiving the person who is. Get the help you need to break away from these unhealthy attachments. Also, understand it doesn't have to necessarily be a "bad" relationship to validate walking away. The relationship may seem to be going well, but if they're not the right person for you, this relationship is bound to take a bad turn eventually. Ask God for the strength to do what is truly best for you, which is walk away.

Further Insight

#1: I haven't been alone in a long time. I have always had a relationship or someone in my life. How do I find the strength to embrace being single and to stop entertaining men that aren't right for me?

First of all, start by being honest with yourself. It can be rough when you have never taken the time to learn how to be by yourself. I recommend you find a support group that you can interact with and gain encouragement from. Support can be found at your church or through a group of friends who share your struggle. Being alone does not mean you will be lonely. This time should be spent identifying and exploring your purpose and the things you are passionate about. The process becomes a lot easier when you are working towards something and engaging in activities that truly connect you with what you need and who God created you to be. As a result you will become more comfortable with yourself and learn to love and like yourself for who you are.

#2: My family is constantly on my case about finding a man and getting married. I'm so sick of it but they just won't stop. How do I deal with this and not allow it to drive me insane or push me to get with a guy that I know I don't truly want to be with?

Your family may have good intentions but their approach typically can be an annoyance and unnecessary pressure in many cases. The best thing to do is be honest about where you are with things in your relationship or why you're choosing not to be in one. Don't just stay quiet and give in to the demands or pressure they are trying to push on you. Let them know how their approach makes you feel and the negative impact it is having or can have on your decisions. Now I know some of you have family members who won't care, like your parents for instance, who just want you married so you can produce them some grandkids. In this case, you just have to practice staying calm, positive, and not buying into what they feel makes sense for you. Again, they won't be involved in your relationship when it's all said and done. When you feel miserable and unfulfilled by the choices you made, they will not take credit for helping you make those decisions. Don't let them get to you, be patient and take your time. Continue to stand your ground on doing what is truly best for you.

#3: I am in an abusive relationship and I don't know how to get out of it. I fear for my life as well as the lives of my kids. What steps can I really take to break free?

It's easy for me or anyone else for that matter to simply say to someone, "just leave", but I know it isn't that simple sometimes. There has been a lot of fear put in place to keep you from leaving and your concerns are valid. I encourage and recommend first and foremost that you pray and seek God during this time. Also, reach out to those around you for support; friends, family, your church family, your pastor or your community. There are many organizations (that can be found online or by calling an abuse hotline) who have years of experience helping women in abusive relationships break free and live better lives. They will be able to provide you with the assistance you need, from transitional housing to counseling and medical attention. Congratulations on taking the first step, which is you recognizing and deciding it's time to walk away! Now you are can begin taking the necessary steps to ensure the safety of yourself and your children. Remember God can make a way out of no way once you decide and act on faith.

You're Too Focused on
What You Want

"If anyone's will is to do God's will, he will know whether the teaching is from God or whether I am speaking on my own authority."

John 7:17

I know what you're thinking. If the person isn't what I want, then why should I have to accept being with them? That's a valid question. We all like what we like and there isn't anything wrong with that. We all have our preferences and we can find plenty of scriptures that essentially instruct us to tell God what we want. Some women of God have even been instructed to make a list of exactly the kind of man they desire and take the list and pray over it with faith God will deliver their man according to their list of wants. So you're thinking, "What could possibly be the issue with this approach?"

A woman I knew had a very specific breakdown of what she wanted in a man. The man she wanted was; a college graduate, with a well paying job, no kids, but would like some, he was at least six feet tall and in good shape. I could continue with the list, but you get the picture. She knew exactly what she wanted. If a man was missing something on the list she wouldn't entertain him at all. She had made up her mind about her dream man, based on her list of desires and she wasn't trying to hear anything else. Well guess what? She actually found a man that matched her list. Initially she was excited because she thought she had found "the one". She felt validated in her approach and had all the bragging rights of proving those wrong who felt she was being too picky and unreasonable in her approach. Life was great, until she realized that he had what she *wanted* but he couldn't provide her with what she *needed*. His *resumé* was great, but he did not provide her with the kind of love that truly spoke to her heart. She was back at square one. She found herself still feeling unfulfilled and confused by the fact that she had this great guy, but there was still something missing and even though he was great, she didn't have the connection with him that she thought she would. She was in denial about it for a long time, but she couldn't shake the fact that the deep genuine feelings just weren't there with this guy no matter how much she wanted them to be.

This happens to women all the time and some stay stuck in a relationship because they don't feel they can validate leaving. He's everything they wanted. What's the problem? They have to come to grips that they received exactly what they wanted and are still unhappy. This is a

> **"...women get so locked into what they want; they overlook the person that's truly best for them."**

very tough pill to swallow. Many women get so locked into what they want; they overlook the person that's truly best for them because they can't see things clearly. I hope you are grasping why you shouldn't focus so much on what you want. Here are some other thoughts to consider:

#1 — Wants Change, But Needs Are Persistent.

What a person wants in high school likely isn't going to be the same when they are in their twenties. It could change again in their thirties and depending on various factors it could change again and again as a person grows and matures. When you focus on what you currently want in a partner today, you could very well be setting yourself up with a partner you will want to get rid of later on. That's why you have to switch your focus to what your true needs are. A woman may want a man to have a minimum salary amount, but what she needs is for that man to have the drive and ambition to provide for their family. A woman may want a man who is a little bit of a "bad boy" but what she needs is man who can be assertive and handle his business while still providing her the love and respect she deserves. God knows best. He knows the man to provide what you need for the long run vs. the man, who is just currently trying to give you what you want right now, that is always subject to change. God knows which man is a smokescreen vs. the man you aren't seeing for who he truly is because there are too many distractions in your way.

#2 — Timing Is Everything.

We want everything RIGHT NOW! Forget all this waiting nonsense. When we feel we are ready, well that should be enough right? Well, God doesn't work on our clocks. He knows when we need more time than we might think to prepare for love and the true relationship we desire and need. Being patient can be difficult but being impatient can prove to be dangerous. God has His own methods and system of doing things. The more we fight them, the more we set ourselves back. When God has a great blessing for you, it usually comes with a process. It may be filled with tests, but when you embrace the process, it will produce for you a great testimony.

#3 — Your List May Not Fall In Line With God's Will.

So back to people in the church telling others to make a specific list of what they want in their partner and ask God to deliver that person to them. Sometimes people will do that, but then end the prayer by saying "God let your will be done". Well, what you have on your list may not be a part of God's will. Yes he can give you exactly what you asked for, but as I mentioned earlier; wants change and needs are consistent. Unless your list is truly based on what you need then it can become a conflict of interest. God knows better than you, so why try to limit His blessing by trying to define it yourself? God doesn't need your help, He needs your obedience. The path He may want you to take to get to your blessing may not involve anything you expected or even want to bother with having to deal with. When you are truly seeking to do God's will, you can rest assured the final result is the best outcome and you will be a much better person at the end of the process.

I always say to clients, "instead of always asking God for what you want, consider asking Him to prepare you for the blessing He has for you." We may think we're ready but there may be plenty of things we're overlooking. God isn't going to hand your Boaz over to you prematurely before you're ready because that situation usually doesn't end well. It's like giving a person a million dollars before they've learned how to manage money.

> **"God isn't going to hand your Boaz over to you prematurely..."**

They will blow through the million and end up in a worse situation than the one they started with. God wants to see us do wonderful things with the blessings He has for us. Be patient with yourself and the process. Be open, and trust that God knows what you need and when you need it, to ensure a spectacular outcome.

Further Insight

#1: So you're telling me I shouldn't hold on to what I want in a man? I should entertain any man that has some potential? Am I supposed to overlook the fact that I am not physically attracted to him because he may be the man I need?

Again, there is nothing wrong with having preferences, but I would encourage you not to overlook a man you genuinely feel drawn to simply because he doesn't fit the specific mold you wanted. Many women have walked away from a man they felt a deep connection with because the situation wasn't exactly how they wanted it to be (too many kids, family pressure, career, etc). This is not the best course of action to take. You don't have to and probably shouldn't entertain a man romantically who you are not attracted to. Being attracted to one another is important. The attraction might not cause you to drool on first glance and the attraction may take into consideration other factors that go beyond just the physical, which makes the attraction richer and more fulfilling. Be able to recognize what you need vs. what you want or you may find yourself getting neither and ending up alone or with someone who isn't truly best for you.

#2: If now is not the time then when? I've been waiting for a long time and I'm not sure I can continue being patient. What if the man for me never appears? Are some of us just destined to be single forever?

Pray and ask God. Remember, it doesn't happen according to our timing, but God's. Some would suggest that you may have a gift of singleness and therefore you should accept that maybe a relationship isn't for you. Personally, I feel only God can confirm this for you. In His confirmation it is likely you would find peace in being single if this truly is the case. Otherwise you probably don't have that specific "gift" and someone may have told you this by default because they didn't know what else to say. You may have been single for a while and I can understand how unnerving this can be. Understand that the hold-up isn't because the man for you doesn't exist but that you may not have been doing the things necessary to clear your path to him. So as difficult as it may be, don't dwell on the time that has already passed. Focus now on moving forward in a positive direction and know that as you embrace being the woman God wants you to be, you will receive the Boaz blessing He has for you.

#3: Isn't it GOD's will to give us the desires of our heart? So wouldn't what we want automatically fall in line with his will?

I believe the true desires of our hearts include things like; love, patience, positive energy, and so on. The things we truly need have already been placed in our hearts by God and those are the things that really sustain us. Do you know of a person who has chased after theirs wants, and then when they get what they desired, they still feel unhappy and unsatisfied? Our wants are temporal and surface. Our wants originate from the mind and are influenced by others. Our needs originate from our hearts and we are taught not to trust them or seek them out because we won't find them. God will give us the desires of our hearts because those desires were given to us by Him and so are within His will. Since we confuse our wants with our needs we misinterpret the meaning of the scripture. This doesn't mean we won't get any of the things we currently believe we want. Sometimes we want what we need. The product of God's will, may come in a different package than what we expected, so it might appear to be different when it is in fact exactly what we wanted and needed.

God's Already Sent Your Boaz,
You're Not Embracing Him

"Blessed is a man who perseveres under trial; for once he has been approved, he will receive the crown of life, which the Lord has promised to those who love Him."

James 1:12

M any women think love is supposed to come easy. They believe if it's "too hard" that means the love isn't meant to be. Personally, I disagree with this belief completely. The ability to catch feelings for a person comes naturally, but the act of loving and being loved, building a relationship and maintaining the love best for you will not always be a walk in the park. The reality is you will come across plenty of resistance when trying to come together with the person and love for you. It makes perfect sense when you think about it. The last thing the Devil wants to see is the two people

God created for each other, actually together. Have you ever noticed how some of the greatest relationships had to initially get past huge obstacles to get there? It's all part of the process and for some women it is an inevitable part, if they ever want to get their Boaz blessing.

That said, some of you already know your future husband, but for various reasons, you haven't taken claim to this fact. Something (or someone) is blocking your vision or has made you unwilling to walk the path necessary to be with him. You try to convince yourself "they're not the one" and you continue to look elsewhere. You may find other men to entertain, but you likely will still find yourself lacking the fulfillment you truly desire in a relationship. You may still be expecting God to throw someone else your way, but why should He? The right person for you is already right under your nose. It's best to acknowledge some of the possible reasons why you're struggling to accept your Boaz:

#1 — True Love Can Be Scary.

To like someone is easy. To lust someone is even easier. To truly embrace the love that is truly best for you is one of the scariest situations a

Stephan Labossiere-*God Where Is My Boaz?*

person can come up against. Not because love itself is a bad thing. God is love, so we should recognize that love is amazing. It's just that when you as woman have seen and experienced so much hurt you likely won't enjoy the idea of having to be vulnerable yet again. That's exactly what true love requires. True love demands our vulnerability. True love is overwhelming and terrifying in many cases and as a result people run from it because they can't control it. It feels *safer* to entertain people we know aren't meant for us. In these types of relationships you maintain emotional control and feel you are less likely to suffer extreme hurt. You know you don't care as much for the random man as you do your *true love*. It seems like the only logical choice when trying to minimize possible heartbreak. However, most likely this plan is contrary to the plan God has for you. It isn't easy, but again you need to ask yourself; "will you let fear (the Devil) or faith (God), guide your decisions?"

#2 — The Circumstances Seem Too Difficult to Overcome.

It can be distance, resistance from family; feeling stuck in a relationship that isn't truly for you, the list of reasons can go on and on of why you're not embracing your Boaz. Faith is; believing in the things unseen. However, when the circumstances in front of you are too overwhelming, you may turn around and run away. The battle appears to be all uphill and impossible and for what? You feel like the relationship holds no guarantee. Especially, if you've already been through a lot in your life, it may not seem worth it to fight through the chaos for the possibility of true love. However, if he is the man God has for you, then fighting is necessary. There will be plenty of good to come from it...even if it doesn't seem that way at first. It's important to focus less on the obstacles and more on the truth behind the deeper connection between you and your true love. If a true connection really exists, you already have a vital part of the foundation needed to conquer this situation. Circumstances are subject to change and they can change quickly. All things considered, is it really worth not embracing who your Boaz is, when God is telling you otherwise?

#3 — He Is Not What You Expected.

You expected a man with a corporate job but instead you find yourself drawn to a physical education teacher who works at your local high school. You wanted a man with no kids who has never been married. He's divorced with two kids by two different women. However, you find your spirit drawn to him even though he doesn't fit your pre-conceived listed criteria. This makes you think twice about moving forward with him. This scenario applies to a lot of women. Many would rather hold on to the type of person they think they want, instead of moving forward with the type of person they know they really need. You have to break free from the limited box you have placed yourself and your potential Boaz in. Being open to the possibilities will allow you to discover your unexpected Boaz blessing.

If you've been running from a love you know exists already in your life, the time has come to stop dead in your tracks. If you've been overlooking the love that you have and know is for you, it's time to adjust your vision. The only way to know for sure is to get into prayer and ask

God directly. If you continue to turn away from the blessing God has presented to you, you will only cheat yourself out of the happiness you truly deserve. Embrace God, embrace true love, and embrace the one man you know God has already revealed to you.

Further Insight

#1: How can I trust love without feeling like it won't come back to bite me in the butt if I embrace it? I thought I was in love before and it ended in disaster. Am I really supposed to trust this man and this relationship will be any different if I embrace it?

God doesn't require you to trust a man, He desires for you to trust Him. Your trust should be in God to protect and guard your heart. He doesn't want you to be reactive and miss your blessing based off of a past experience and fear. There is no guarantee this man may never hurt you or make any mistakes. There may be moments where he lets you down and you are left a little disappointed. When God says he is for you, this is still the person you need to be with. Again, put your trust in God and not the man.

You will experience much more love and happiness that will far outweigh any down moments. You may have thought you were in love before, but was that based on what you thought or did you honestly go to God to make sure it wasn't another fleeting emotion? Chances are you were using your own logic to base your understanding of things at that time, but now you're going to do it God's way and with his guidance. You can rest assured it will not have the same outcome and this love will not bite you in the butt. Remember what the bible says on the matter, *"Perfect love, casts out all fear." 1 John 4:18*

#2: I've been dealing with a guy long distance for a while now. I really do love him but everyone is telling me I am wasting my time. We aren't sure yet when we will be able to be in the same place. So am I fooling myself by trying to hold on?

If you know this is the man for you then you aren't fooling yourself by trying to hold on. You just have to make sure you are taking the best approach while trying to get through this time of distance between you. Long distance relationships are hard work and you have to make sure you both are on the same page about your needs and plans. If you feel this isn't the case, it might be best to embrace friendship while you continue to work on yourselves and prepare for the time you both can come together in the same place. Don't try forcing the relationship because if the timing isn't right this can create bigger issues. Be patient and allow yourself to embrace what you know God has in store for you when the time is right.

#3: What if I believe my Boaz is a close friend? Would it really be wise to cross that line with him? I love him but I don't want to ruin the friendship we have.

There are a lot of women who are in this predicament. Crossing the line with a friend to explore a loving relationship is a very difficult decision to make. As a result many women chose not to despite their true feelings. As hard as it may be you will only keep yourself in a negative cycle by not embracing the love God has for you. You do run the risk of losing your friend if things don't work out, but you also have the wonderful possibility of exploring true love with someone you already care about and trust. It's best to be open and honest about your feelings for your friend to eliminate any confusion that may arise

Stephan Labossiere-*God Where Is My Boaz?*

from your feelings. Allow things to progress as they need to and always be willing to openly discuss any concerns now that he knows how you feel.

God Wants You to
Focus More on Him

"But seek ye first the kingdom of God, and
his righteousness; and all these things shall
be added unto you."
Matthew 6:33

When I was looking for a scripture to
add to this section I chose the one
above. It seemed to the best fit, but
as I dug a little deeper, the scripture which hit
home for me was; *"If any [man] come to me, and
hate not his father, and mother, and wife, and
children, and brethren, and sisters and his own life
also, he cannot be my disciple."* Luke 14:26

Whoa! I mean that sounds pretty harsh. The
use of the word hate shocked me at first, but I
feel it wasn't being used in the way we know it to
be used normally with the negative connotation
attached. I could be wrong, but what I took from
it was the premise; you should always be prepared
to leave anyone, including loved ones for God. He

comes first and should never play second in our lives. To some extent this is a hard pill to swallow for most, but it says a lot about where our focus should be, which is on God.

It's a beautiful thing to see two people experience true love together. It's definitely something we need to see more of in this world. We know we're supposed to put God first. It's biblical, but does that really happen in real life? Not practically. We love God and we put forth a conscious effort to express our love for Him in various ways, but we usually always have room for improvement. It's very easy for us to become blinded by our desires and to not realize the things taking a higher priority over God. It's extremely normal to think we're on the right track, when we're actually off our path completely. So much so that we're not sure we have the right directions at all. God wants our attention, our time and our love also. Sometimes we behave like a child fixated on TV. When our parents come through the door, we don't even acknowledge them. We have to check ourselves. We can get our focus back to the right place

(God) by correcting some of these common mistakes:

#1 — You're Putting Your 'Boaz' Over God.

Everybody loves to be loved and sometimes the desire to have love consumes us. At times you may become completely fixated on achieving love either with the person already in your life or the thought of the man who you have yet to meet. You think about "him" constantly and it may cause you to lose track of what is truly important; cultivating your relationship with God first. Can you imagine what God thinks as He watches us put Him on the back burner for the other things we want that we are relying on Him to give us? He probably says to himself, "why that ungrateful piece of..." Ok, maybe He isn't thinking that at all, but you get the point. He needs us to keep our eyes on Him and when we do, He takes care of the rest.

2. You Have Religion but You Do Not Have a Relationship.

You may be thinking, "I focus on God. I read my bible. I'm celibate (some of you have only been celibate for 3 days but at least you're trying and you have to start somewhere), and I go to church every Sunday. What do you mean I don't have a relationship with God?" Well, just because someone walks into a church building, doesn't necessarily mean they're truly walking with God. Following certain religious practices on the surface, doesn't compare to embracing true spiritual growth from within. None of us are perfect and making certain efforts to live right and go to church is good and commendable. We just shouldn't overlook taking the time necessary to truly connect with God. Understanding we need to focus more on building a relationship with Him and not with religion. When we get our spiritual relationship in line with God, we position ourselves to receive the romantic relationship we desire in our lives.

#3 — You Are Not Following Instructions.

There are many cases where you know God has spoken to you and instructed you on things you should do. It could be in your career, family life, in your spirituality, or love life yet you have struggled to carry out the orders He's given. It happens to the best of us and I'm as guilty as anyone. Sometimes what God tells us to do feels scary, confusing, or we simply feel like it's too much for us to deal with. However, when we overlook the instructions, we still look for our desired blessings. Well there is a path God wants us to walk and on that path our blessings are laid out waiting for us. We have to take steps forward and go get it by doing the things He's *instructed* us to do. God wants to make sure the time is right for us to receive the person He has for us, but it also requires our willingness to embrace the path He leads us on.

Again none of us is perfect. Most, if not all of us, have had moments when we took our eyes off God. This might be the reason why we got hit upside our heads by life. The great news; today is a new day! We can always adjust our focus and start seeing straight. It's all about continuing to put forth effort to move in the right direction. We will most likely fall again, but we can get back up and try to learn from our mistakes. The more we allow ourselves to grow in the process, the more we become who we were called to be. As a result we can receive the person that was called to be with us. What does this mean for you? Your Boaz!

Further Insight

#1: Yes, I do want the husband God has for me, but I don't feel like I have put that over God. I'm trying to do my best to be the woman God called me to be. So how do I know if I've crossed that line of putting my desire for a man over God?

Here are two questions to ask yourself if you're not sure you're putting God first:

Do you spend more time dwelling on the man you don't have vs. thanking God for the blessings He's given you? If so, you might be putting that man over God.

Are you still trying to get your man by your means? Rejecting God's direction on how He wants you to handle the situation? If so, you are putting that man or your desire for him over God.

Our desires can become distracting when we obsess over them. You might not even realize you're obsessing over him until someone else points it out. For example, a woman may put her new man over her purpose driven career. She may not realize it because of her natural enthusiasm to spend time with him as much as possible. One day one of her friends flat out calls her out on it. She will either admit she's wrong and acknowledge she needs to correct the action with striking a better balance or deny it and disregard her friend's observation about what's going on. Take a moment to honestly evaluate your actions to determine if you are indeed falling into this trap without realizing it.

#2: If I'm reading my Bible and going to church doesn't that mean I am building a relationship with God? What could I possibly be overlooking?

I want you to picture having a man who spends time with you, but doesn't really interact with you. He does what he thinks he's supposed to do on the surface, but he isn't really connecting with you and bonding with you on a deeper level. His actions are out of obligation because you've told him what you want. Deep inside he hasn't truly embraced this desire you have and why it's important for him to want you the way you desire him to. Well, to some extent this describes how some people treat their relationship with God.

They can go to church, read the bible, but still not have a relationship with God. They know of Him, but do not know Him. It's important and wise for us to go deeper and connect with God on a spiritual level. Simply talking to Him in prayer helps a lot and truly embracing His principles in your life will also help.

#3: I've felt that God instructed me to do certain things and I didn't listen. Time has passed and I wonder if I missed my opportunity. Is it really too late or should I just do what I felt God told me long ago?

It's never too late to start walking in obedience to what God has told you to do. I recommend you go into prayer to find out what currently needs to be done. It may be the same instructions He gave you before or it may be a different plan He has for you to follow, but that will ultimately get you to the same goal. Don't dwell on mistakes you've made in the past. Learn from them and take a better approach today and from where you are now. The blessings God has for you don't go away. They just remain waiting for you on the path He wants you to take to receive them.

Conclusion

You're probably wondering how so many other women with these same exact issues, have still been able to overcome them and find their Boaz. Things are not always what they seem. When people ignore God's guidance or don't properly seek out God's guidance, they always pay a hefty price for it. Sometimes they pay the price immediately. Other times the consequences are delayed or are not always seen by others. One way or another, the results don't turn out well. People aren't always honest about their struggles. They smile in your face and claim all is well, little do you realize, their home life is a war zone and negativity has taken over their relationship. Don't get caught up in what you perceive other people as having. You don't know what they had to go through to get it and you don't know the ongoing price they may have to pay to keep it.

As tough as it may be to accept some of the things I mentioned in this book, it's in your best interest to face your issues. Running from your issues won't make them go away. Trying to stay distracted, won't save you from the damage the unresolved issues will continue to cause in your relationships and in your life. To overcome any obstacle, you have to acknowledge the cause of the issue and face it head-on. You have to take the necessary step(s) to move forward and conquer it. Unresolved issues will not go away in time by themselves and nobody can remove them for you. You will have to look within yourself and seek God's direction if you truly desire the most effective way to eliminate them completely.

You may be saying to yourself, "but why do I have to deal with this now" or "why can't God just remove it for me and let me be done with the issues altogether?" Here is the answer to both of these questions; there are lessons to be learned and you can't grow unless you go through the trials, experience the lessons and embrace them for what they are. The things we go through in life and in our relationships help build our character and strength, when we fight through them. The lessons also give us the experience and knowledge we need to help others who may walk a similar path. We build an appreciation for all the things God brings us through as we overcome each obstacle by His grace. When we are constantly handed what we want without putting in any work, we don't know how to value the blessings as they should be valued. We start to take things for granted and may neglect the purpose of the blessing and why it's been given to us. The trials God allows us to go through are for our own good in the long run. It may not seem like it at the moment but with every test there is an opportunity for a testimony. Also, look at God as a teacher. He allows us to retake tests over and over again, no matter how many times we've failed before. We always have a chance to finally pass. Just know the test is not going anywhere and you can't move forward until you actually do what is necessary to pass it.

Ultimately, I hope this book helped shed light on any issues that may have been hindering your growth and blocking you from receiving your Boaz. Everyone has issues, but using them as an excuse, ignoring them or acting as if they aren't important will not make them disappear or help your cause. The path God has for you isn't always the easiest, but it's always the most rewarding. Stay strong, stay faithful, and stay connected to the one that can lead you to everything you deserve and more, God.

The End

For more answers to your relationship questions or for other resources to help you along on your journey visit me at:
www.stephanspeaks.com.

For in-depth relationship analysis and life coaching contact me directly by email:
contact@stephanspeaks.com.

Questions & Answers

1. If I follow the suggestions you present in this book, how quickly can I expect to get a man?

The results will vary. I have had discussions with women who immediately saw a breakthrough. Whereas with others it took some time before they were with their Boaz. Others are still going through the process. One thing for sure is that taking heed to the message in this book will place you on a more positive path and move you much closer to your Boaz blessing.

2. Is it possible the issue is that men are just ridiculous and don't know a good woman when they see one?

I agree that many men are still not where they need to be in life and do not always understand the value of a great women. I would still say that this should not be the focus of a woman who is

GOD WHERE IS MY BOAZ?   91

still waiting to get the man she deserves. I have yet to work with a woman that was not able to pinpoint very important issues that were hindering her from receiving her blessings.

3. Why is the focus always on women and what they need to do? What about the men, why aren't you telling them about themselves?

Society does tend to focus more on the women but that isn't my goal. I actually have written a version of this book for men as well. They need as much advice if not more than women do and I understand that. My first book, *How to Get A Woman To Have Sex With You...If You're Her Husband* was written to try to help men understand how they can be better men for the special women in their lives. So I will always do my part to address everyone and help both men and women move in a more positive direction.

4. I know God wants us to save ourselves for marriage but that isn't always easy or desirable. Does engaging in sex eliminate my chances of finding the guy God has for me?

I won't say it eliminates your chances, but it certainly makes it much more difficult. Many women get distracted or too attached when in a sexual relationship with men and make it harder for them to realize he isn't for them. Sex can cloud your judgment and hinder your ability to address the deeper issues which exist. Nobody is perfect but I do think it is in a woman's best interest to fall back from sexual activity and take time to focus more on herself and God.

5. I'm celibate and I'm ok with that but it doesn't seem like men feel the same way. Can I really expect to get the man for me when so many are focused on having sex?

Absolutely! I agree that a lot of men are focused on sex but I have seen the biggest man whores open to waiting, when they truly felt they found the woman for them. Women just have to understand that it may take some time for that man to see that you are that woman. Most men will not view you that way because you are not the woman for them and there goal all along was sex. This is why building friendships is a great route to take. It allows time to learn each other and see if a true connection exists. Without any expectation of sex or any obligation other than a genuine friendship that may evolve into something more.

Points to Remember

1. Prepare and position yourself.

You have to embody the role of the wife you want a man to see you as and then make yourself seen so that you can receive the man for you.

2. Let faith, not fear guide you.

God doesn't want you operating out of fear. Faith should be your guide and true love should be your fuel.

3. Just because he's a good guy doesn't mean he is the *right guy* for you.

You need a deeper connection than deep like in order to sustain the love and type of relationship you desire. Look deeper than a man with a great *resumé.*

4. Be open to all of love's possibilities.

The man for you may come in an unexpected way or in an unexpected package. Be open to embrace him the way he is and don't block God's blessing because of a few minor alterations which will prove best for you in the end.

5. Don't run from love, run to it.

Running from true love will only rob you of the love you truly deserve. God wants the best for you, and you should embrace love and believe you deserve it.

6. Forgiveness and healing are necessary.

If you don't properly address your past hurts you will continue to experience pain in your present relationships. Forgiveness is a process and healing is a process. Take the necessary time to complete both.

7. All that matters is what God has to say about it.

At the end of the day God knows better than we do. Trust in Him and always seek his guidance first concerning matters of the heart and in all of your relationships.

About the Author

Stephan Labossiere is a man on a mission, and that mission is to make relationships happier and more fulfilling. As a certified relationship coach, a speaker and author, Stephan seizes every opportunity to help both men and women overcome the challenges that hinder their relationships. From understanding the opposite sex, to navigating the paths and avoiding the pitfalls of relationships and self-growth. Stephan's relationship advice and insight helps countless individuals achieve an authentically amazing life. Stephan empowers millions to take charge of the difficult situations standing in the way of the life and love they seek and to make impactful changes on a daily basis.

Dedicated to helping, and devoted to *keeping it real.* Stephan's straightforward, yet compassionate delivery style, attracts a versatile clientele including; notable celebrities, civic and social organizations, academic institutions, singles, and couples alike, who can and are ready to handle the truth!

Seen, heard and chronicled in national and international media outlets including; the *Tom Joyner Morning Show, The Examiner, ABC*, and *Huffington Post Live*,to name a few. Stephan is highly sought-after because he is able to dispel the myths of relationship breakdowns and obstacles—platonic, romantic, and otherwise with fervor and finesse.

To coin a phrase by an individual who attended one of his speaking engagements, "he's definitely the relationship guy, all relationships all the time."

With an international following of singles and couples alike, the name Stephan Labossiere is synonymous with breaking down relationship barriers, pushing past common facades, and exposing the truth. It is this understanding of REAL relationships that he brings to everyone he encounters.

If you enjoyod *"God where is My Boaz"*
be sure to sign up to my email list here
http://bit.ly/IEnjoyedGodWhereIsMyBoaz

You can also follow me on
Twitter & Instagram: **@StephanSpeaks**
or find me on Facebook under
"Stephan Speaks Relationships"

Other Books by
Stephan Labossiere

He Who Finds a
WIFE

A Man's Guide To Finding
The Woman & Love He Desires

STEPHAN LABOSSIERE

He Who Finds a Wife
www.hewhofinds.com